The
STONEHENGE STORY

An Excursion through

Time, Myth and Mystery

Romy Wyeth
Illustrations by Brian Lewis

"Stone gallows"

Brian Lewis

To appreciate Stonehenge properly it needs to be approached leaving the twentieth century and its modern expectations behind, and viewed through the eyes of our imagination.

Too often Stonehenge is looked at in isolation, but it is part of a rich prehistoric landscape which is the most important in Britain. All around on the horizon we can see round barrows or tumuli, the individual burial mounds of the generations responsible for the sarsen circle of Stonehenge. There are 360 recognizable round barrows, another 130 that can only be seen from the air and fifteen long barrows, the earlier neolithic communal burial mounds within a three mile radius of this site. These barrows would have been kept clear of vegetation and the white chalk mounds would have dominated the prehistoric sky line.

Stonehenge is the jewel in the crown, it is a miracle of engineering and a testament of faith left by people long gone, whose memorial in stone has outlived civilizations. In telling the story of this place I will bring together the threads. Most booklets concentrate on part of the whole, this book will incorporate the facts and the legends, the history and the magic. It will I hope be a beginning ....

A henge has two meanings; in the archaeological sense it is a bank and ditch enclosure, found only in Britain. The German word *hengen* means a gallows or a hanging place. In both of these contexts Stonehenge qualifies. The first stage, some five millenia ago was a bank and ditch enclosure, and the great Sarsen Circle, called in legend 'The Giant's Dance', resembles a stone gallows. Sometime between 3,000 BC and 2,800 BC the first stage of the monument began. It was a great, circular bank, six feet high with an opening in the direction of the sunrise. The ditch, unique in a henge enclosure, was outside the bank. It may have had practical rather than ritual significance, and its purpose solely that of a quarry for the chalk mound.

Inside the bank was a circle of 56 post holes, with a diameter of 284 feet (86.7 m). Some of these holes had cremations in them, added at a later date, but this was not their purpose. The cremations may have been a way of sanctifying the site, bringing the ancestors of the builders to the new religious enclosure.

56 is a number that equates very well with lunar or solar calculations. It is possible that the movements around the skies of the sun, the moon and the planets were plotted by placing markers in the post holes, having charted their orbits over the

six-foot-high bank, which would have provided a false horizon. Accurate calculations over the real horizon would have been far more difficult.

These holes are called the Aubrey Holes after their discoverer, John Aubrey, who was commissioned by Charles II shortly after the Restoration to survey Stonehenge and Avebury. In 1666 he mentioned seeing cavities within the bank. Another theory is that they may have had a ritual significance. If so we can only speculate what it may have been; as with so much at Stonehenge the truth is shrouded in the mists of millenia of time.

The four station stones have in the past been placed at the first phase of the monument. The four points intersect at or very near the centre of Stonehenge. One line is aligned on the most southerly moonrise and another on the most northerly moonset.

The Heel Stone, or Sun Stone, (from the Greek *Hlios* meaning Sun) has also been placed within the earliest phase of building but current archaeological thinking is that it is unlikely that just a few stones were on site a thousand years before the rest of the sarsens appeared. The first stage probably contained a wooden building in the centre of the henge, traces of timber were discovered during the most recent studies of the site in 1995.

In legend the Heel Stone is so called because it is said the Devil picked it up and threw it at a friar and it hit him on the heel, leaving a permanent mark.

The only unworked stone on the site stands 256 ft (78m) from the centre of Stonehenge, in isolation by the side of the road. Today it is leaning towards the monument; it was in the beginning upright – it weighs 35 tonnes and would have needed 250 people to transport and erect.

Traditionally the sunrise on the longest day, 21st June, is said to be directly over the Heel stone. It isn't, – it is slightly to one side. The earth's axis has shifted since the monument's construction but this would have meant that the Summer Solstice sunrise would have been further to the west. It is possible that there were originally two of these stones, the socket of a second stone having recently been discovered, and that in prehistory the sun shone between them. The sun will rise directly over the Heel Stone in AD 3260 – in another incarnation you may see it but not for another twelve centuries.

A series of post-holes were discovered in an area near the

Opposite: Heel Stone and Slaughter Stone.

Brian Lewis

opening of the Henge bank, close to the Slaughter Stone. They cannot be seen, but it is important that their presence be noted, because they represent six years worth of calculations five thousand years ago. Not earth years, but lunar ones, and as each lunar year is 18.61 years, we are talking about 111 years of observations. Three to five generations at least would have passed before the research was completed. The manner of their alignment suggests they were annual markers to record the most northerly positions at which the full moon nearest to midwinter rose. This would have made it possible to discover the nineteen year orbit when the phases of the moon repeated themselves, the so called metonic cycle.

In the car park there are three circular marks running from east to west. These, together with an unmarked post-hole in the area of the pay kiosk are the oldest post-holes on the site. Around 8,500BC there is evidence that these holes contained huge pine posts. Archaeologists believe that these could have been the totem poles of the hunter-gatherer people who roamed the landscape ten thousand years ago. Astronomers have suggested they could also have been used as far sighter alignments, one lining up on the summer solstice sunset and another on the moonset from the Heel Stone. The site would appear to have been in continuous use from the time the Henge Bank was built until its abandonment 1,500 years later.

The Bluestones

The next phase began with the arrival of the Bluestones, somewhere around 2,400 BC. These stones, weighing up to four tonnes, were sacred to the Beaker people, so called for the distinctive pottery found in their graves. The Beakers were responsible for the stone stages of Stonehenge; they were in prehistory between 2,400BC and 1,800BC, a transitional people between the end of the New Stone Age and the beginning of the Bronze Age. They were travellers who sought metals, and the Preseli mountains of South Wales had special significance for them. These mountains, 130 miles from the monument site, were the source of the Bluestones, which came from ten sites within an area of a few kilometres. There is reason to suppose that some of them were erected in a circle elsewhere, either in Wales or on Salisbury Plain, before their final resting place was reached.

To reach the Plain it is thought the stones travelled a 240 mile journey, by raft or dugout from Wales up the Bristol Channel and then on the rivers of southern England to Salisbury, and along the Wiltshire Avon to West Amesbury, the closest to Stonehenge that there is any water.

The theory that the stones arrived naturally, during the glaciation period of the last Ice Age has been discarded. If the glaciers brought them they were remarkably selective and brought no other foreign stones as they moved across the prehistoric landscape. Some bluestones have reportedly been discovered on the river beds along which they would have travelled, seemingly evidence they did come by water and that some of the rafts sank en route. For some reason this stage of building was never completed, a double circle of postholes were dug but the Bluestones were erected in a double three quarters of a circle, and then taken down to be used at the final stage of the monument.

The Sarsens

Four thousand years ago, possibly as early as 2,300BC, the great sarsen stones made their appearance on the site and Stonehenge began to emerge, as far before the birth of Christ as we are now after the event. The stones came from the Marlborough Downs twenty miles away. They are a type of sandstone and are also known as grey wethers. It is believed that the word 'sarsen' is derived from 'Saracen'. In the twelfth and thirteenth centuries in Europe, during the Crusades, the Saracens were the strangers, the sarsen stones were the stranger stones.

This stone has a high surface resistance to abrasion, on Mohs scale which measures this, diamonds are ten, steel is 6.7 and sarsen stone is 7. The only tool that was available to dress and work the stones was sarsen stone itself. Round balls of stone, of various sizes, known as hammer stones or mauls were used, and the enormous effort of rubbing stone against stone, often only discarding dust particles, would have begun. The stones were roughly dressed at source and then dragged to the monument, probably on a form of sledge or on rollers. Archaeologists have calculated that it would have taken a thousand men seven weeks to move one stone, and fifteen hundred when they were travelling uphill. It is estimated that ten years was needed to bring more than eighty stones to the site. It should be noted that, like icebergs, there is a great deal unseen beneath the surface, and that the uprights have between four-and-a-half-feet and six feet of foundation beneath the chalk.

A circle of thirty uprights was erected, with thirty lintels making a continuous circle on the top, and in the centre five great trilithons, their size making it likely they were in place before the outer ring was built. A trilithon is two uprights with a lintel across the top, they were horseshoe or bulls horn-shaped, and opened in the direction of the sunrise. The first two were 20 feet high, the second pair 21 feet high and the central trilithon 24 feet high.

No one knows if the number has any significance, but one theory is that they were meant to represent the five tribes of the Wessex Chieftains who were powerful Plains dynasties with great flocks and herds. They traded in weapons and bronze tools manufactured on the continent, and into their graves they took the evidence of their wealth: pottery, weaponry, jewellery and sometimes tools. Another, that Stonehenge was sepulchral and the trilithons compared to a five chambered cairn. The theory I prefer which ties in astronomically, and also if I am honest because it is more romantic, is that they represent the five planets that can be seen with the naked eye in the night sky – Mercury, Venus, Mars, Jupiter and Saturn. Here we are indulging in conjecture and fantasy for as the twenty first century approaches, the Stonehenge people recede ever further from our understanding.

When the sarsen stones arrived, pits were dug in the chalk with the antlers of red deer. Radio carbon dating only works on living matter, and the fragments of red deer antler found in the pits have been used to establish the time scale. The earth was carried away in the shoulder blades of cattle, and about two hundred men with the use of rollers, ramps, levers and ropes would have been needed as the stones were hauled upright until the centre of gravity tipped the uprights into place. The bases were then packed with earth and discarded mauls; the sarsen stones allowed to settle and possibly left with a certain amount of movement to aid the workers align the stones more easily when the lintels were being placed in position.

The lintels, which weighed up to seven tonnes, were raised in one of several different ways. The first possibility is that blocks of wood were placed at either end of the lintel as far up as could be reached. Then a timber platform was built, the blocks were raised again and the scaffolding built up again in stages until the top was reached.

A second theory is that ramps were built and the stones pulled up them. If this is the case the ramps were of timber and not of earth – the plain was much more heavily timbered four thousand years ago and wood was readily available and far more portable than earth. The archaeologists tell us there is no evidence

Brian Lewis.

of any excavation at this time. (A third possibility was put to me by an American tourist who said I had it all wrong and that the lintels were put in place by levitation!)

But still the job wasn't finished, because on the top of each sarsen stone is a tenon – at least two of the uprights show these clearly. All the sarsen stones had mortise and tenon joints; added to that the outer circle of lintels also had tongue and groove joints. Imagine the effort it took to rub away until all that was left was a small lump of stone. So we have carpentry joints in stone; the first henges were of wood and they did not survive, but this one, the great henge, remains one of the wonders of the world.

All of the stones were shaped and smoothed, tapering in at the top, the lintels delicately curved. The best and smoothest faces of the stones are towards the inside – this was a place that was meant to be viewed from the centre. When the monument was complete it looked perfectly symmetrical, which is why, when it was first discovered, it was thought to have been a temple built by the Romans when they occupied Britain for four centuries within forty-three years of the birth of Christ. When it was realized that it was ancient when the Romans arrived, John Aubrey, out

Opposite: 'The Heart of the Sanctuary'.

of his burning desire to find an answer to its purpose, wrongly concluded it was built as a Druid temple. This has caused the archaeologists problems for three hundred years, so entrenched in the public mind has this become.

The Druids did not come into existence until a thousand years after the monument was complete; they did not build it and it is unlikely that they ever worshipped there, preferring to perform their rituals in groves of trees, near running water.

In the ditch between the stone circle and the Heel Stone is the totally misnamed slaughter stone. Because it was found laying with iron ore stains visible it was thought to be a bloodstained, Druid, sacrificial stone and given its evocative name. It was in fact one of a pair or even three stones, the ceremonial entrance way leading into the circle. The remaining stone is the largest of the Trilithons, with its great tenon, weighs fifty tonnes and has foundations eight feet deep. In 1220 medieval craftsmen built Salisbury Cathedral on foundations of only four feet, beneath which is shingly shale. The spire and the tower weigh 6,400 tonnes. Here in prehistory a 32 feet sarsen stone was erected and a quarter of its length hidden beneath the chalk.

Opposite: The largest stone – part of the great trilithon.

Brian Lewis

The Conclusion

The final stage of Stonehenge was completed by 1,550 BC. The Bluestones had been reintroduced, a complete circle of Bluestones was placed between the outer sarsen circle and the inner sarsen horseshoe created by the five great Trilithons. Within this sarsen horeshoe yet another horseshoe, this time of 19 Bluestones was added. In addition, the so called altar stone, a micaceous sandstone from Pembrokeshire, was placed inside the Bluestone horseshoe. The stone stood alone facing the sunrise at the heart of the sanctuary. Its name probably arose because, when one of the uprights and the lintel of the great trilithon toppled, they fell onto the micaceous sandstone and it now lies beneath them. Subsequent visitors who saw the micaceous sandstone prostrate on the ground assumed from their Christian heritage that they were looking at an altar. It was originally upright and not laying down as its present position suggests. More post-holes, known as the X and Y holes, have been found, they were dug after the sarsen circle, and are outside it; their purpose is unknown.

The Builders

The period of the stone stage of construction at Stonehenge covered approximately 800 years – imagine how many generations lived and died before the final phase was complete.

The round barrows arose at about the same time as the stone circle and these individual burial mounds are obvious in the landscape, even today. Whether the groupings are tribal or family we don't know. Archaeologists believe the mounds may also have been used as territorial markers, establishing continuity of lineage.

The peoples of Stonehenge do not appear to have lived there; their settlements were elsewhere on the Plain and they gathered for festivals or rituals on the site at various times of the year. The debris found at the monument is the kind left from ceremonial feasting rather than everyday living.

They had stopped being hunters and wanderers and become farmers. Now the seasons were important to them but, if all they needed was a basic calendar or observatory, the first henge monument would have been sufficient; they did not need to go to such lengths as today we realise they did.

Imagine the manpower needed to move the stones; the massive labour force would need to be spared from the work in the fields and surplus food and clothing provided. Great effort was needed to dig pits in the chalk with only antlers, engineering skills to erect and place the sarsen stones and time to smooth and shape the stones having hauled them from their sources. This was a

Brian Lewis

communal undertaking on a huge scale and the motivation for such an exercise must have been powerful indeed.

All activity on the site appears to have ceased shortly after it was finished. To have abandoned a sacred area that they had laboured on for such a period of time some drastic change must have taken place. Perhaps the bottom fell from their economy and they were forced to relocate, maybe a great plague came and they were wiped out or did invaders from across the sea massacre the population? Whatever catastrophe befell the Stonehenge peoples, they disappeared from history almost at the moment their great achievement was perfected. The site became overgrown and forgotten, to reappear in recorded history after the Roman invasion.

Alignments

The most famous alignment at Stonehenge is the sunrise at the summer solstice, but it would appear to the worshippers that the important alignment was the midwinter sunset. The Avenue consists of two parallel banks, it was the Processional or Ceremonial Way, arcing through the gap in the trees to the north-east and

Opposite: Slaughter stone in the foreground – the ceremonial way is facing the midwinter sunset.

21

into the monument beside the present Heel Stone, through the ceremonial gateway, with the sunrise alignment at the back of the worshippers. They would be facing the greatest Trilithon in the centre, which would frame the midwinter sunset through a portal made of stone. To a people who were attuned to the earth the days that followed the winter solstice would bring the sun back from its death throes to rebirth and renewal.

The Legends

So what really is this great temple of the plains? To the medieval peoples the stone circles were sometimes rumoured to be sinners who danced on the Sabbath and were turned to stone.

In the legends of King Arthur it is said his Druid magician Merlin magicked the stones from Ireland, some say by air, some by water and some that the Devil brought them, to place over the grave several hundred British nobles, slain in the fifth century by Hengist, a Saxon invader. The story goes that they were buried in a mass grave on Salisbury Plain.

The legends of the Mediterranean tell of an island in the west where a great circular Temple to the Sun God Apollo stands. And if you have read Erik Von Daniken's *Was God An Astronaut* you may be forgiven for wondering if in prehistory we were visited by beings from another planet who constructed Stonehenge as a sighting point around the earth.

The monument was reputed to be the site of healing rites in the past. Spring water was poured over the stones and then believers washed in the charged water to cure their ailments.

At various periods of our history the pagan circle was the target of religious bigotry. During the English Civil War it is said the Parliamentary army was encouraged to go to Stonehenge and to try to destroy it by lighting fires beneath the stones and then pouring cold water over them to aid efforts to damage the circle.

New Theories

In his book, *The Stonehenge Solution,* George Terence Meaden suggests that the monument was a pagan fertility Temple built on the site where Cosmic Consummation was commemorated. He says that the double horseshoe of Trilithons and bluestones represented the womb of the Mother Goddess, and the stone known as the altar stone, in effect the Goddess stone, stood on what was viewed as the centre of the world, the axis which united Heaven and Earth.

Dr Meaden's theory is that throughout June the sun shines onto the Heel Stone, sending the shadow like a giant phallus entering the circle and the horseshoe, representing the union of the Sky God with the Earth Goddess.

Brian Davison, the former Stonehenge archaeologist, believes Stonehenge was built as a ruin. His theory is that the first Henge monument included a bank and ditch, the Aubrey holes and, in the centre, a sacred wooden building. When the Beaker people arrived they discovered rotting timbers from the sacred building and replaced them with the more enduring stones which have survived for more than four thousand years.

The Facts

Many Bluestones disappeared when early tourists stopped at the blacksmith's shop at Amesbury to hire a hammer and chipped away their own souvenirs. Treasure hunters searching beneath the sarsen stones also contributed to the destruction. What do we really know about Stonehenge? We know where the stones came from, the people responsible for the building, possibly the methods used and, thanks to the radio carbon dating of the deer antlers found in the pits, the approximate dates. Where, who, when and how – these questions we can attempt to answer. What, however, is more difficult.

The Druids

Stonehenge is not a Druid Temple, despite the popular myth. However, the Druids may have had the answer to the purpose of the stone circle. They were the Shamen of the people, the historians, the wise men,the genealogists, and their tradition was an oral one. The Druids were a caste rather than a priesthood, and initiates spent twenty years in forest sancturies and caverns learning the ancient lore, which is thought to have been in verse.

The Druids were known for their wisdom; they officiated at religious and magic rituals. They had a religious awe of fire and water, a reverence for the number 3, and used ritual weaponry and sacrifice. They also had knowledge of astronomy, of calendars and of the nineteen-year metonic cycle.

Maybe they were aware of the purpose of Stonehenge. Nothing was written down but the oral tradition was passed on down the generations. However, when the Roman Occupation of Great Britain began in 43 AD, the Druids were politically a nuisance to the legions – they were a focus of British resistance and so they were hunted to extinction, and with them died the only chance of knowing for sure the secret of Stonehenge.

A Sacred Landscape

It is believed Stonehenge had to have a religious and spiritual significance. We know little of the beliefs of the Stonehenge peoples; archaeologists have suggested for all we know they could have been born dead. We have their burial mounds, their grave goods and their stone circles. As farmers, the yearly cycle would have been vital to their survival and we think that the earth was seen as a living entity represented by a Goddess figure. A carving on one of the great trilithons, said to be the mother goddess, has been found. Carved four thousand years ago, before the sarsen stone was erected, this could be an indication of the religious purpose of the circle. Other carvings, of axe heads and a Mycenian type dagger, have also been found; these possibly date to the final stage which was completed by 1550 BC.

It is suggested by archaeologist Brian Davison that when the monument was completed a head high bank could have been intact so that it act as a screen, protecting the sacred rituals inside the circle from the eyes of those not initiated in the mysteries. The priests and the chieftains were those who could have been participants in the ceremonies; the builders probably were excluded from the temple once it was completed.

Midsummer sunrise at Stonehenge

Stonehenge is at the heart of a sacred and a ritual landscape, surrounded by the graves of the elite of prehistory. If the stone circle can be seen as the hub of a wheel, there are solar and lunar alignments which go through the centre like the spokes of a wheel. The kind of alignments found at Stonehenge are the kind that would have been the result of prolonged observation rather than mathematical precision, as has sometimes been suggested.

The history of dowsing in the West Country can be traced to the fifteenth century when German dowsers came to England to locate lost tin mines. Condemned by Martin Luther as being the work of the Devil, dowsing has nothing to do with the black arts. Eight out of ten people can dowse to varying degrees; it has nothing whatsoever to do with belief. In my opinion, it depends on body chemistry. A form of energy beneath the earth that we are unable to measure scientifically is transmitted through the body and into the rods. It is possible at Stonehenge to pick up the alignments in a vehicle and even on the top of a double decker bus. It is not recognisably magnetic because although many people use metal welding rods bent for hand holds, others use wood while pendulums of all descriptions also react strongly.

If you take dowsing rods and walk around the circle the rods move on the alignments, many of which are sited at the openings between the stones. At Carnac in Brittany, where huge avenues of stones are arranged in lines across the French countryside, the stones appear to be standing on top of the energy lines. It seems highly unlikely this could be accidental. The four station stones, or the Aubrey Holes, are sited where markers were placed as the monument evolved. Today it is possible to discover by dowsing a form of earth energy, as yet unknown, which may explain part of the mystery as to why Stonehenge is in such an apparently inauspicious place. Much has been made as to why ancient peoples brought the bluestones 240 miles from a place already sacred to them, and the sarsen stones twenty miles to the site. It would have been far easier to construct their circle close to the source of the materials, so why did they choose to haul the stones to a waterless site where they themselves never settled? Perhaps they did so because they recognized that this is a place of strong earth energy, earth forces, earth magic – call it what you will. The ancient Chinese called it the dragon power and the earth energy lines (today we call them ley lines) the dragon paths. One of the legends of Stonehenge said it was a sacred place of Dragon or Serpent Worship.

Is it coincidence the area is also in myth connected with Uther, the father of King Arthur? Vortigern, whose nobles were slain by Hengist, was rumoured to have been involved in the murders of both King Constantine – Uther's father and Uther's eldest brother – King Constans. The second son was Aurelius Ambrosius (after whom nearby Amesbury is supposedly named), who revenged these murders by killing Vortigern, and is reputed to have placed a worthy monument over the grave of the massacred Britons. Legend says this was Stonehenge. Constantine's third son was Uther, who took the name 'Pendragon', or 'Dragon's Head'.

Before the Henge appeared in prehistory the ancient Chinese were practising acupuncture. This recognises two opposite and complimentary energies, which can be found in all of nature, flowing along pathways known as meridians.

The ley lines have been compared to the veins beneath the surface of the earth mother and there is a school of thought that suggests that the Stone pillars act as acupuncture needles penetrating the earth's energy centres, which channel and strengthen strong earth places.

Stonehenge is reflective and it mirrors the beliefs, the dreams and the expectations of those who travel from distant places to

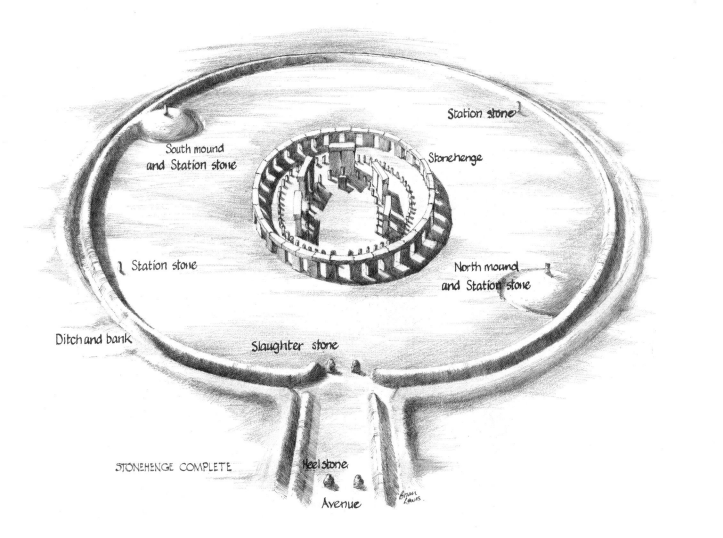

Station stone

South mound
and Station stone

Stonehenge

Station stone

North mound
and Station stone

Ditch and bank

Slaughter stone

STONEHENGE COMPLETE

Heel stone

Brian Lewis.

Avenue

an inhospitable and exposed grassland in Wiltshire. It is a testimony to man's practical ingenuity and spiritual longings, and a place of mystery, of magic and of enduring wonder.

*   *   *   *   *

Explaining Ley Lines

The old Saxon word *ley* (also spelt lea, lee or leigh) was defined in the *Oxford English Dictionary* as 'Land temporarily under grass' and particularly refers to an enclosed field or pasture.

The first person to use the term as we think of it today was Alfred Watkins in his book *The Old Straight Track,* published in 1925 when he was seventy years old. Alfred Watkins lived in Hereford and on leaving school became an outrider or brewer's representative which meant that he covered large areas of his native countryside around the Welsh borders.

Watkins noticed that traditionally sacred sites such as burial mounds, standing stones, earth works, beacon hills, and churches built on earlier pagan sites often seemed to be arranged in straight lines. His original interpretation of this seemed to be that these were prehistoric sight lines across the landscape; today we think of them more as earth energy lines. Dowsing on the markers placed by ancestors distanced from us by millenia of time has shown these spots have strong earth energies.